Acknowledgments

To everyone who helped create this thorough guide, I would like to extend my deepest gratitude. Your unfailing assistance, wisdom, and experience have been crucial in transforming this information into a useful and educational resource.

I would like to express my sincere gratitude to my mentors, whose advice and experience have been crucial in forming my grasp of the subjects covered. Your commitment to spreading knowledge is sincerely admirable.

I also want to thank all of the writers, researchers, and teachers whose efforts have improved the information in this guide. Your dedication to advancing knowledge has motivated me to delve deeply into these topics.

I'd like to express my gratitude to my friends and family for their support, tolerance, and faith in my capacity to do something worthwhile. Your steadfast encouragement has served as a steady source of inspiration.

Finally, I want to express my gratitude to the readers who interact with this tutorial. The motivation for producing educational content is your curiosity and drive to learn, and I feel privileged to have contributed to your quest for knowledge.

I appreciate you all.

Esther Campbell

Table of contents

Acknowledgments

Chapter 1.	Financial Education
Chapter 2	Setting clear goals
Chapter 3.	Budgeting
Chapter 4	Spend Less Than You Earn
Chapter 5	Emergency Fund
Chapter 6.	Debt Management
Chapter 7	Prudent Investment
Chapter 8.	Continuous Education
chapter 9	Entrepreneurship
Chapter 10	Long-Term Mindset

Conclusion

Chapter 1

Financial Education

Making informed and empowered decisions about money management, investing, and reaching long-term financial objectives all start with financial education. It gives people the information and abilities they need to successfully negotiate the complexity of personal finance and create a stable financial future.

An extensive description of what financial education comprises is given below:

Basic financial literacy: It's important to comprehend basic ideas like income, expenses, budgeting, savings, and debt. You can build a strong financial foundation and make wise financial

decisions if you are financially literate

.

Learn how to make and stick to a budget in this lesson on budgeting and money management. Make sure you're living within your means by keeping track of your income and categorizing your expenses. You can allocate money to savings, investments, and other financial objectives with the aid of a budget.

Learn the value of consistently saving money in the section on savings and emergency funds. Creating an emergency fund offers protection against unforeseen costs and financial losses.

Understanding different debt forms, interest rates, and strategies for managing and lowering debt are all part of good debt management. More of your money can be available for saving and investing if you learn how to efficiently prioritize and pay off debt.

The fundamentals of investing: Learn about the several types of investments available, including stocks, bonds, mutual funds, real estate, and retirement accounts. Learn about diversification, risk and return, and long-term investment tactics.

Understanding compound interest is important because it enables your money to increase rapidly over time. Understanding compound interest can motivate you to begin investing early.

Learn about employer-sponsored retirement plans (such as 401(k)s), individual retirement accounts (IRAs), and Social Security when it comes to retirement planning. Find out how to calculate your retirement requirements and make a plan to reach your retirement objectives.

Tax Awareness: Recognize the fundamentals of taxes and how they affect your earnings, assets, and financial choices. Find out how to invest tax efficiently and how to reduce your tax liability.

Risk management and insurance: Learn how insurance can help you secure your financial security. Learn about several insurance options, including life, health, auto, and house insurance, and how they contribute to financial stability.

Learn about wills, trusts, and estate planning to make sure your assets are dispersed as you intend and to reduce the possibility of taxes and legal entanglements.

Learn about common biases that can influence financial decisions and other psychological aspects of money management in this course on behavioral finance. Create plans to help you make wise financial decisions.

Continuous Learning: Keep abreast of evolving economic trends, investment opportunities, and financial trends. Think about reading books, going to workshops, and getting your financial news from reliable sources.

Chapter 2

Setting clear goals

An essential first step to success, particularly in the area of personal finance, is the establishment of specific goals. Your financial journey has direction, motivation, and a roadmap when your goals are well established.

Here is a thorough description of how to formulate specific financial objectives:

Decide What You Want to Achieve Financially:

Start by deciding what you want to accomplish financially. Your objectives may be to fund your children's education, buy a home, pay off debt, save for retirement, or take a dream vacation. Each objective will have a different time frame and budget needs.

Be Specific: Each objective should be carefully stated. For instance, instead of just stating, "I want to save for retirement," be more specific about when you'd like to retire and how much you'd like to have saved.

Quantify Your Objectives: Assign a monetary value or measurable indicator to your objectives. This provides you with a specific goal to strive for. Find out how much you'll need for a down payment, for instance, if purchasing a home is your objective.

Establish Timelines That Are Realistic: Create a schedule for completing each objective. Think about both immediate and long-term objectives. While long-term objectives like retirement planning may take decades to complete, short-term objectives may be accomplished in a year or two.

Prioritize Your Objectives: Sort your objectives according to their significance. Ascertain which objectives need to be completed as soon as possible and which ones can wait. This aids in the efficient allocation of your time and energy.

Large goals should be broken down into smaller, more attainable milestones if they appear daunting. This increases the goal's reachability and makes it possible for you to monitor your development over time.

Create Measurable Objectives: Establish standards that will enable you to gauge your development. For instance, if paying off credit card debt is your objective, establish concrete monthly or annual goals for doing so.

Include a Why: Recognize the motivations behind your aspirations. Knowing why a certain goal is significant to you can inspire you and keep you steadfast when things get tough.

Take into account your financial limits by taking an honest inventory of your situation. Make sure your objectives can be met in light of your income, expenses, and other commitments.

Review and adjust your goals frequently. Over time, priorities may change, there may be life changes, or there may be changes in the economy. Review your objectives frequently and adapt as necessary.

Create a mental or physical image of your objectives to help you visualize success. You can increase your drive and maintain your attention by visualizing your success.

Celebrate Your Success: When You Achieve A Milestone Or A Goal, Take Time To Celebrate. Giving yourself a reward motivates you to keep working toward greater goals and reinforces good financial habits.

Chapter 3

Budgeting

A crucial financial tool that supports effective resource allocation, money management, and goal achievement is the budget. It entails coming up with a strategy for how you will make, use, and save your money. Here is a thorough budgeting manual:

Evaluation of your financial situation

Start by assessing your present financial situation. Determine your overall income, taking into account your salary, wages, and any other sources of revenue.Identify your typical outgoing costs, including those for housing, utilities, groceries, transportation, insurance, and entertainment.Sort Your Expenses into Groups:

MONTHLY BUDGET '23

MONTH :

	INCOME	
DATE	SOURCE	AMOUNT

	BILLS	
AMOUNT	DUE DATE	PAID DATE

	EXPANSES	
DATE	SOURCE	AMOUNT

	SUMMARY	
	SOURCE	AMOUNT
Income		
Expances		
Bill to Pay		
Summary		
	Total	

NOTES

RECORD   BOOK

Decide which expenses are stable (consistent each month) and which are variable (fluctuating).Set housing, utilities, groceries, and debt repayment as top priorities.Establish a Budget:

List your income and expenses using a spreadsheet, a budgeting tool, or a pen and paper. To determine your net cash flow, subtract all of your expenses from all of your income.Set financial objectives.

Include both your immediate and long-term financial objectives in your budget. Set aside money for debt repayment, investments, savings, and other specific goals.Maintain a Spending Log:

As you spend money, keep track of it. You can automatically categorize and track your spending with the aid of many budgeting applications.To make sure you're remaining within your budgeted boundaries, periodically evaluate your spending.Refine and Adjust:

Regularly review your budget and make adjustments in light of evolving conditions, such as shifting income or unforeseen spending.Emergency Reserve:

Set aside money from your budget to create an emergency fund. Try to save three to six months' worth of expenses in case of unforeseen financial difficulties.Investments and Savings:

Set aside money from your budget for investments and savings. Retirement accounts, brokerage accounts, and other investment vehicles may fall into this category.Repayment of Debt:

If you have debt, set aside money from your budget to pay it off over time. Pay the minimum on other obligations while concentrating on high-interest ones.Regular Review:

Review your budget frequently to make sure you're on course. Adjust as necessary to keep your expenditures in line with your financial objectives.Behavioral Elements

Be aware of your spending patterns and actions. Steer clear of impulsive purchases and adhere to your spending strategy.Communication:

Ensure open communication about budgeting objectives and spending choices if you share your finances with a partner or family members.

Follow your budget consistently over time in order to experience favorable financial returns. Better financial health can result from making budgeting a habit.

Celebrate Your Successes: As You Go Along, Celebrate Your Successes Recognition and motivation are due for reaching financial or budgeting milestones.

Chapter 4

Spend Less Than You Earn

An important financial principle is to live within your means, which entails not spending more than you make. It's a key idea for attaining monetary stability, lowering debt, conserving money, and ultimately increasing wealth. Here is a thorough description of how to live within your means:

Mindset Change:

You must change the way you think about and handle your money if you want to adopt the "live below your means" mentality. Focus on making wise financial decisions rather than trying to keep up with lavish spending or lifestyle inflation.

Save More Than You Spend:

Your overall spending, which includes both necessary costs and discretionary expenses, should be less than your overall revenue. As a result, there is a rise in the difference between your income and outgoings.

Budgeting:

Living within your means requires careful planning and budgeting. Make a thorough budget that lists all of your income and outgoing costs, making sure to include funds for debt repayment, investments, and savings.

Establish a distinction between bare necessities (shelter, utilities, groceries, and healthcare) and luxuries (eating out, entertainment, and luxury goods). Put needs first and consider wants carefully before spending.Stay away from lifestyle inflation.

Avoid the urge to quickly raise your spending as your income rises. Instead, put the extra money into investments and savings to advance your financial objectives.

Saving Money:

Adopt thrifty behaviors by looking for affordable alternatives and making thoughtful financial choices. To make the most of your money, keep an eye out for sales, discounts, and coupons.Put investments and savings first.

Spend a sizable amount of your salary on investments and savings. Creating an emergency fund, funding retirement accounts, and purchasing long-term assets are a few examples of how to do this.

Reduce Debt

Living within your means allows you to put more money toward debt repayment, hastening the process of getting out of debt.

Experiencing Rewards Later:

Practice delayed gratification by delaying immediate indulgences in favor of accomplishing longer-term, more important financial objectives.

Security and liberty:

Living within your means gives you financial security and independence. You'll feel more at ease knowing that you can handle unforeseen costs and have the money to achieve your objectives.

Growth in Compounds:

Compound interest grows your money over time when you continuously save and invest, which can greatly accelerate your wealth building.

Avoidance of Financial Stress

Living within your means lessens financial strain and the need to borrow money or use credit cards to pay bills. This helps to enhance one's mental and emotional health.

Financial LongTerm Objectives:

residing within your means aligns your spending patterns with your long-term financial objectives, such as supporting your children's education, early retirement, property, travel, or early retirement.

Regular Self-Evaluation: Review your spending patterns on a regular basis to make sure you're adhering to the idea of living within your means. Make changes as required to keep a sound financial balance.

Chapter 5

Emergency Fund

A vital financial safety net, an emergency fund gives you a buffer to meet unforeseen costs, financial setbacks, or emergencies. It's an essential part of a comprehensive financial strategy that gives you peace of mind by making sure you have enough money to cover unforeseen expenses.

A thorough explanation of an emergency fund is provided below:

What an emergency fund is used for:

An emergency fund acts as a safety net against unforeseen financial needs such as medical costs, job losses, automobile or home repairs, or other unanticipated bills.When faced with unexpected expenses, it keeps you from having to rely on credit cards, loans, or long-term investments.

Establishing the Fund

Start by deciding on a certain amount you want to save for your emergency fund. Generally speaking, financial experts advise saving three to six months' worth of living expenses, but your particular situation may require a different goal.

How to Calculate Expenses

Calculate your monthly important expenses, such as those for housing, utilities, groceries, transportation, insurance, and debt repayment, to establish your emergency fund goal.

Beginning Small:

Start modestly if saving for a sizable emergency fund seems daunting. Start small with your monthly donations and progressively increase them as your financial situation improves.

Easily attained and liquid

Store your emergency fund in a highly liquid and accessible place, like a conventional savings account, a money market account, or a different checking account.

Account Dedicated To:

To resist the temptation to use the money for things that are not necessary, set up a special account for your emergency fund.

Contributions:

With each paycheck, consistently add money to your emergency fund. Automate the procedure to guarantee consistent deposits.Setting the Emergency Fund's priorities

Investment in your emergency fund should come before other financial objectives like debt repayment or investment.

Substituting Withdrawals:

If you do need to spend money from your emergency fund, try to replace it as soon as you can.

Adapt Depending on the Situation:

When circumstances in your life change, review and modify your emergency fund objectives. Your financial needs may be impacted by significant life events like marriage, having children, or purchasing a home.

Comfort of Mind:

Knowing that you are equipped to face unforeseen financial difficulties without jeopardizing your long-term financial objectives gives you peace of mind.Economic stability:

Your overall financial security and stability are improved by having an emergency fund, which also helps you feel less stressed and concentrate on your long-term goals.Alternative Savings vs. **Emergency Fund:**

In contrast to other savings objectives (such as retirement or vacations), an emergency fund is created exclusively to meet sudden and unexpected financial demands.

Review and reevaluation:Review your emergency fund on a regular basis to make sure it reflects your needs and financial condition. Make any necessary alterations.

Chapter 6

Debt Management

Debt management is a calculated strategy for managing and reducing debt while upholding overall financial stability. It entails coming up with a strategy to manage current debts, cut down on interest expenses, and work toward becoming debt-free. A thorough discussion of debt management is provided below:

Determine Your Debts:

Making a list of all your debts, including credit cards, loans, mortgages, and other outstanding sums, is a good place to start. Keep track of the interest rates, required minimum payments, and overall balances for each. Make debt a priority.

Based on interest rates, order your debts. To reduce the amount of interest you'll pay over time, give paying off high-interest bills top priority.

Establish a Budget:

Create a thorough budget that lists all of your costs and your monthly revenue. Spend more money on debt repayment while making sure to pay for necessities. Cut back on new debt.

Avoid taking on additional debt whenever you can while concentrating on paying off current obligations. Only use credit cards sensibly and for essential purchases.

Avalanche vs. Snowball Method

Use the debt snowball approach to pay off the smaller bills first to gain momentum, or the debt avalanche method to pay off the debts with the highest interest rates first to save money on interest more quickly.

Interest rate negotiations:

Make contact with your creditors to discuss better terms or reduced interest rates. The overall cost of paying off your debt might be dramatically decreased with a lower interest rate.Loans for consolidation:

Investigate the possibility of combining many loans with high interest rates into one with a lower interest rate. This can streamline payments and possibly result in cost savings.

Strategy for Paying Off Debt:

Choose a debt management strategy—the "debt snowball" or "debt avalanche"—and stick to it religiously. Celebrate each loan that has been paid off to stay motivated.recurring payments:

Set up minimum payments and additional contributions to be made automatically. Automating payments helps avoid late fines and missed deadlines.

Further Payments:

Whenever possible, put more money toward your debt with the highest priority. Over time, even a tiny increase in payments can have a big impact.

Emergency Reserve:

Keep a separate emergency fund to meet unforeseen costs, so you won't be forced to use credit cards or loans in the event of a financial disaster.

Look for Expert Assistance:

Consider obtaining advice from a credit counseling organization or a financial counselor with knowledge of debt management if your debt situation is dire.

Track Progress:

Keep tabs on your debt-reduction progress frequently. Observing your debt balances drop might boost your drive by making you feel accomplished.

Mark Important Occasions: Salute your progress and accomplishments. Financial freedom is one step closer with each loan that is paid off.

Chapter 7

Prudent Investment

Making strategic and well-informed decisions to manage risks and increase your wealth over time is part of investing properly. It's crucial to reaching financial objectives and safeguarding your financial future. Here is a thorough guide to making sensible investments:

Learn for Yourself:

Take the time to educate yourself about the various investment possibilities, asset classifications, risk factors, and market trends before you begin investing. The secret to making wise decisions is knowledge. Specify your investment objectives.

Establish your investment goals, whether they are to achieve financial independence, save for retirement, buy a home, or pay for your children's school. Your investment plan will be influenced by your objectives.

Risk Acceptance

Recognize your capacity for and willingness to withstand changes in the value of your investments. Your asset allocation choices will be influenced by your risk tolerance.

Diversification:

To lower risk, diversify your investments across many industries and asset types (such as stocks, bonds, and real estate). Your portfolio can be protected through diversification from the effects of a single underperforming investment.

Time Frame:

Take into account how long you intend to keep your money invested—your investing time horizon. You might be able to take on greater risk and possibly achieve larger returns if you have longer time horizons.

Asset Management:

Invest your money in a variety of assets based on your objectives, risk tolerance, and time horizon. Your overall investment strategy should be in line with your asset allocation.

Investments in research:

Investigate potential investments in great detail. Examine past performance and financial statements, taking into account elements including economic and market trends.

Investment Instruments:

Select suitable investment vehicles, such as equities, bonds, mutual funds, exchange-traded funds (ETFs), real estate, or retirement accounts like IRAs and 401(k)s. Fees and costs

Be mindful of the expenses related to your investments, such as transaction costs, taxes, and management fees. Keeping costs to a minimum will help you increase profits.

Stay Up to Date:

Keep up with market changes, economic news, and financial news that could affect your assets.

Avoid Investing Emotionally:

Instead of acting on impulse or in response to short-term market volatility or emotions, base your judgments on logic and long-term objectives.

Examine and correct:

Review your investment portfolio frequently to make sure it stays in line with your objectives and risk tolerance. As your circumstances change, make adjustments.

Consult a professional.

Consider consulting a certified financial counselor if you're uncertain about investing or have complicated financial goals.

Patience and self-control

Patience and discipline are necessary for successful investing. Instead of pursuing quick profits, concentrate on your long-term investing plan.Start out strong and keep it up.You can increase the value of your investments by staying in the market for a long time. Start saving early, make regular contributions, and let compound interest work for your benefit.

Chapter 8

Continuous Education

Throughout your life, you can continue to learn new things and develop new abilities and perspectives by engaging in continuous learning. It's a proactive strategy for your professional and personal growth that will help you remain current, adjust to change, and improve your all-around abilities. Here is a thorough manual on lifelong learning:

Mindset for Lifelong Learning:

Accept the idea that learning continues after formal education. Recognize the need for ongoing learning for developing personally, advancing professionally, and adjusting to a world that is changing quickly.

Stay Inquisitive:

Develop a passion for information and a sense of curiosity. Even if they are outside of your comfort zone, be open to learning more about new topics and concepts.Set Learning objectives.

Establish precise learning objectives and goals. Setting goals gives your learning efforts direction, whether they are focused on developing a new talent, learning about a particular industry, or discovering a new passion.

Informal and Formal Education:

To increase your knowledge, take advantage of both official (courses, workshops, and certifications) and informal (books, articles, podcasts, and internet resources) learning opportunities.

Structured Education:

Enroll in educational opportunities that relate to your interests or line of work. Numerous courses on subjects ranging from technology to the arts are available through online platforms.

Self-Directed Education

Take the initiative to study on your own. Using books, articles, YouTube tutorials, and other online resources, research and investigate topics of interest.

Maintain Current:

Being current is essential in fields that are continually evolving. Read industry magazines frequently, keep up with thought leaders, and go to conferences or webinars.

Discussion and Networking

Network and participate in discussions with peers who have similar interests to yours. Join online communities, participate in forums, and go to meetups to share expertise.

Utilize Learning:

Use the knowledge you gain in practical circumstances. Practical application improves comprehension and aids in retaining new information and abilities.

Consider and Review

Review what you've learned from time to time. Think about how it has affected your life or career and how you may use your knowledge even more effectively in those areas.

Resilience and Flexibility:

Your resilience and flexibility will improve as you continue to study. It gives you the tools you need to confidently face new difficulties and make adjustments.

Gaining Professional Experience

Continuous learning helps people stay employable and develop in their careers. Gaining new abilities and expertise can lead to job opportunities and advancement.

Personal Development

Your life is improved and expanded through learning. It encourages personal development, builds self-esteem, and improves your capacity for deep discourse.Managing your time and your balance

Strike a balance between your other activities and your ongoing education. You may devote time to learning while still attending to other obligations, thanks to effective time management.Set a good example:

Encourage others to embrace continuous learning by embracing it yourself. This will serve as an example for others, including your kids, coworkers, and classmates.

chapter 9

Entrepreneurship

The process of starting, growing, and running a company with the intention of introducing novel concepts, goods, or services to the market is known as entrepreneurship. Entrepreneurs take calculated risks in order to address issues, meet needs, and add value. Here is a thorough guide to starting a business:

Generation of Ideas

Finding a business idea is frequently the first step in entrepreneurship. Personal experiences, market gaps, new trends, or technical advancements can all serve as inspiration for this concept.

Market analysis

Perform in-depth market research to comprehend your target market, their wants and preferences, and the market environment. Verify the practicality and potential demand of your proposal.

Business Strategy

Create a thorough business plan that includes your mission, objectives, target market, value proposition, marketing plan, financial forecasts, and operational strategy.

Creativity and innovation

Creativity and innovation are essential to entrepreneurship. Look for distinctive ways to set your product or service apart from those of the competition.

Risk evaluation

The hazards associated with entrepreneurship include commercial, operational, and financial hazards. Create backup plans to help you mitigate any hazards you identify.

Finance and Funding:

Decide how you will fund your company. Personal savings, loans, venture money, angel investors, crowdfunding, and grants are among the possibilities.

Business Organization:

Select a business legal structure, such as a corporation, LLC, partnership, or sole proprietorship. Every structure has effects on governance, liability, and taxation. Producing a product

Focus on designing, prototyping, testing, and fine-tuning your product if you're selling one. To enhance the features and functionality of the product, collect feedback consistently.

Marketing and branding

Create a compelling brand identity and marketing plan to successfully advertise your company. Use both online and offline means to connect with your target demographic.

Distribution and Sales:

Choose the sales and distribution channels for your product or service. Online sales, collaborations with merchants, or other channels of distribution may be included.

Acquisition and Retention of Customers:

Deliver value and top-notch customer service to draw in and keep customers. Create long-lasting connections and promote repeat business.

Building a team

You might need to work with partners or hire staff as your company expands. Create a strong staff with complementary abilities to support the operations of your company.

Learning and Flexibility:

Entrepreneurship necessitates adaptation and ongoing learning. Be willing to change your strategy as necessary, keep an open mind to criticism, and keep an eye on market trends.

Financial Administration:

Uphold sound financial management procedures, such as reliable record-keeping, cash flow management, and budgeting.

Scaling and expansion:

As your company grows and prospers, think about scaling and expanding. This could entail opening up new markets, releasing fresh merchandise, or franchising.

Chapter 10

Long-Term Mindset

A long-term mindset is a way of thinking and acting that prioritizes long-term objectives, steady growth, and postponed gratification. It entails making decisions and acting in ways that put long-term outcomes ahead of short-term desires. Here is a thorough manual for developing a long-term perspective:

Goals and Vision:

Whether they pertain to your work, relationships, health, or finances, develop a clear vision of your long-term ambitions. Establish long-term objectives that are relevant and reachable in light of this vision.

Experiencing Rewards Later:

Practice holding out on rewards now to get bigger rewards later. Recognize that making sacrifices today can result in subsequent results that are more noteworthy.

Consistency and Patience:

Accept the virtue of patience. Recognize that reaching important goals requires patience, perseverance, and regular activity. Despite obstacles, maintain your resolve and perseverance.

Time Frame:

Instead of thinking in terms of days or weeks, shift your perspective to include years or decades. Think about how your present activities will affect your future selves.

Decision-Making:

Rather than focusing on immediate benefits, base judgments on their long-term effects. Before making a decision, weigh the prospective advantages and dangers over time.

Investment in Education

Spend time and energy learning new things that will advance your career and personal development over the long term.

Planning your finances:

Create a thorough financial strategy to help you achieve your long-term objectives. To accumulate wealth and financial security, give priority to saving, investing, and responsible spending.

Wellness and Health: Make good choices that will benefit your long-term wellbeing. Future quality of life will be improved by consistent exercise, healthy eating, and good self-care.

Creating Connections: Develop deep, long-lasting connections. Spend time cultivating relationships that will assist you and ultimately improve your life.

Resilience and Flexibility: Recognize that obstacles and challenges are a necessary part of the trip. Develop resilience and adaptability to overcome challenges and carry on working toward your long-term objectives.

Reflection and awareness: To stay mindful and focused on your long-term goals, practice mindfulness. Consider your progress frequently, make any adjustments to your plan, and commemorate achievements.

Avoiding Temporary Trends: Keep yourself away from passing trends or easy fixes. Make decisions that will benefit your long-term wellbeing and have lasting value.

Greener Alternatives: Take into account how your choices may affect society and the environment. Make decisions that advance a responsible and sustainable future.

Impact and Legacy: Consider life after your own lifespan. Take into account the legacy you want to leave behind and the influence you can have on future generations. A balanced viewpoint

While keeping the long future in mind, strike a balance to take pleasure in the here and now. Keep in mind to treasure your experiences, connections, and momentary pleasures.

Conclusion

Adopting a long-term perspective is like orienting our aspirations' compass toward the horizon as we go through life. It's a conscious decision to put persistent progress, lasting accomplishments, and a profound sense of fulfillment ahead of transitory urges and fleeting pleasures.

We unleash the ability to purposefully shape our future by fostering this mindset. We develop the ability to face challenges head-on, sow knowledge seeds that grow into wisdom, and build enduring bonds with others. The road to postpone gratification becomes one that is lined with planning, perseverance, and the hope of a better day.

The long-term perspective enables us to weave the threads of our dreams into a rich tapestry of achievements, much as a skilled artist creates a masterpiece with painstaking strokes. It serves as a lighthouse, pointing the way through the maze of decisions we face in life and serving as a constant reminder that every action we take today adds to the masterpiece that is our life.

Let us keep in mind that even though the journey may be difficult, the rewards are boundless as we fix our eyes on the faraway horizon. The long-term perspective turns ordinary events into stepping stones for great accomplishments, turning our lives into tales of fortitude, development, and influence.

If you adopt a long-term perspective, every choice you make, every objective you pursue, and every obstacle you conquer will leave a lasting impression on history and inspire future generations. So let's maintain our composure and keep our gaze set on the horizon as we forge a future that is both amazing and durable.